# how to have fun making birdhouses and birdfeeders

## By Editors of Creative

## Illustrated by Nancy Inderieden

DEDICATED TO
TOM, MIKE, KRISTY and TIMMY

creative
craft
book

Copyright © 1974 by Creative Educational Society, Inc. International copyrights reserved in all countries. No part of this book may be reproduced in any form, except for reviews, without written permission from the publisher. Printed in the United States.

Library of Congress Number: 73-10463
ISBN: 0-87191-271-6

Published by Creative Education, Mankato, Minnesota 56001. Distributed by Childrens Press, 1224 West Van Buren Street, Chicago, Illinois 60607

Library of Congress Cataloging in Publication Data
Creative Educational Society, Mankato, Minn.
    How to have fun making birdhouses and birdfeeders.
                (Creative craft books)
    SUMMARY: Lists the necessary tools and materials and gives instructions for constructing birdfeeders and birdhouses for a variety of birds.
    1. Bird-houses — Juvenile literature.   2. Birdfeeders — Juvenile literature.   [1. Birdhouses.   2. Birdfeeders]
I. Title. QL676.5.C7   639'.97'82   73-10463
ISBN 0-87191-271-6

# ABOUT BIRDS

Watching birds is a very interesting hobby. And, since there are about 9,000 different kinds of birds throughout the world you will see birds of many different sizes and colors. Did you know that penguins and chickens were birds?

You can also enjoy birds by just listening. It's fun to try and guess what kinds of birds you hear.

We can find birds in every part of the world. In the United States each state has its own state bird. Do you know what your state bird is? We can also find different kinds of birds at different times of the year. Many birds fly south each winter to escape the cold.

If you want to learn more about birds so that you can name the birds you see, look in the encyclopedias or bird guidebooks. You probably know what a robin and sparrow look like but if you study these birds for awhile, you will learn many interesting facts about these common birds.

After you have spent some time watching and listening, try to guess the name of the bird you are watching or listening to. There are many things that will help you to identify the kind of bird. These are the size, shape, color and pattern of feathers, songs, calls and movements. Keep a notebook of the birds you watch.

# LET'S BEGIN

Birds like to eat. In fact, the smaller the bird is, the more it will eat. Ornithologists, scientists that study birds, say that some baby birds even eat close to their own weight in food in one day.

One way to learn more about birds is to set up a birdfeeder. You will want to find a place for your birdfeeder that will be close to one of your windows. Also, you want to put your birdfeeder where it is easy for you to fill each day. But, remember that the birds are shy. If the feeding box is too close to your window, or in your window sill, it might take a while for them to get brave enough to try it out. Be sure that your birdfeeder is high enough so that the cats will not be able to hurt the birds.

Birdfeeders are very easy to make. They can be very simple, or they can include bird baths and even a roof. Birds do not care what the birdfeeder looks like. They are more interested in what kind of food you have for them. Also, they will come to your feeding station faster if it is not in a cold, windy location.

Another way of watching birds is by building birdhouses. You can build houses that will attract only the kinds of birds you want in your yard. When you are hanging your birdhouses, be sure that they are in the right places for the kinds of birds you want.

Both your birdhouses and birdfeeders should be put high enough so that the squirrels and cats cannot hurt the birds.

Let's start by making some very easy birdfeeders.

# EASY BIRDFEEDERS

A birdfeeder can be made from so many things. Look around your house for something that you can use. It must have an edge on it to keep the food from falling off when the wind blows. And, it must be sturdy enough to withstand the rain, wind or snow. Do not use anything that will become too hot for the birds when the sun is out. A few of the things that you can use are listed below:

Wood—almost any kind

Styrofoam—this is easy to work with

Boxes—A shoebox cover or stationery box cover can be covered with left over scraps of contact paper.

Paper Plates—can be covered with left over scraps of contact paper.

Large plastic covers—like the ones from the gallon ice cream pails.

To hang your birdfeeder use a very strong string or rope. You can wrap yarn around the string or even wrap a string of popcorn around it to help attract the birds.

# Milk Carton Birdfeeders

You can make two kinds of feeders from milk cartons. Both are very simple. First, wash out your milk carton. For the first feeder, cut the carton down so that you have only about an inch left all of the way around. If you want to hang this feeder, put a hole in each side of the carton and hang with yarn or string. You can also put this birdfeeder on your window sill. Just put a couple of nails in the bottom of the box and it is attached.

Or, stand your milk carton up. Tape or staple the top shut. Cut out a small window. This should be close to the bottom of the milk carton leaving most of the top closed. Put holes in both sides of the top part of the milk carton. Run your yarn or string through and hang.

# A Popsicle Stick Birdfeeder

You will need 24 popsicle sticks for the bottom of the birdfeeder. Glue 12 of them together one way and 12 of them together the other way across the top of the first layer. Then, glue three or four on each of the sides to keep the food from falling out. Now glue the popsicle sticks one on top of the other for the back. You can make it as high as you want it. Then make a roof the same way you made the bottom part of the feeder. Now you are ready to paint or decorate your birdfeeder. Try gluing macaroni seeds on the roof and watch what happens. Put a nail in the roof. Hang with yarn or string.

# Mobiles for Birds

Mobiles are fun to make and very easy. So, let's make some mobiles for the birds to eat. You will need one of the plastic boxes that mother gets strawberries or tomatoes in from the store. Take the berry box and cut the bottom of the box off. You will also need one of the sides. Now make a string of popcorn. Attach the two pieces of the box together using the string of popcorn. String from the top of the box as many of these as you want. You can even make other strings with cranberries, suet or macaroni for the birds to eat. Hang your mobile from the clothesline or a tree branch. You can also use a coat hanger for your mobile. Make strings of popcorn and wrap around the hanger. Then, make other strings with berries and attach to the top part of your hanger. Hang from a tree branch or clothesline.

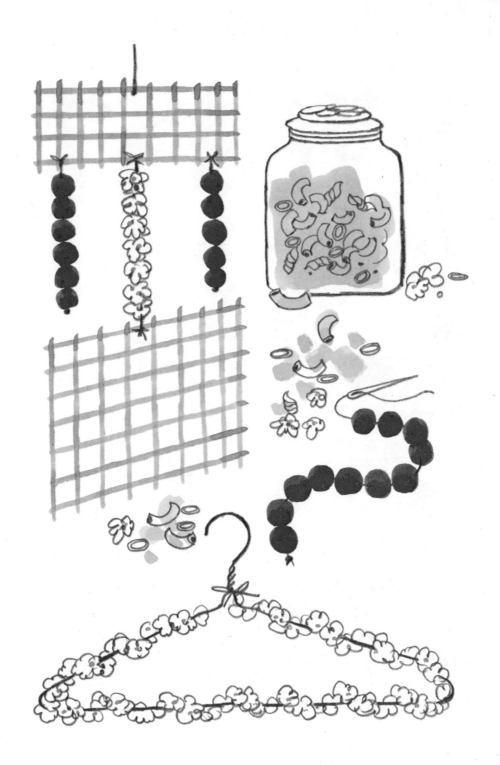

# EASY BIRDHOUSES

Birdhouses are not hard to make. They should be made out of wood. Do not use tin or metal as this will become too hot from the sun. Also, do not put up too many birdhouses in one area as the birds do not like a lot of neighbors. Try to put your birdhouse where squirrels and cats will not be able to get at the baby birds. Also check the encyclopedias and guidebooks to be sure that you are putting your birdhouse in the right place. Some birds like houses near the ground and others like houses very high in the trees.

After a bird family leaves your birdhouse be sure to remove the old nest and clean it out. Each spring you will be able to watch a new family of birds move in, grow up and fly away.

The following birdhouses are listed by birds. Any wood scraps that you find in your dad's workshop will work. Another idea for building some of the smaller birdhouses is to use popsicle sticks.

# A Robin Birdhouse

Robins do not like a closed birdhouse. They like to have a shelf type birdhouse. This is very much like the birdfeeder. Three sides should be open. The floor of the birdhouse should be 7" long and 7" wide. The back should again be 7" high and then should have a roof on it.

# A Woodpecker Birdhouse

Woodpeckers like something that is hollow inside. You could even use a log and hollow it out. It should be about 9" long. Have one single hole and be covered with a roof. The hole should be about 2".

# A Bluebird Birdhouse

Bluebirds like to have their houses where other birds cannot get at them. They should be placed on a clothesline pole or some other pole. It should be placed about 5 feet off the ground. The bottom of the birdhouse should be 5" x 5". The front side 8". The back side 13" high. Make the other two sides 10" high. The top of your birdhouse will slant towards the front. It should be 7½" long and 8½" wide. The hole should be in the front and should be about 1½".

Let's make the next two birdhouses from popsicle sticks. First, let's make a birdhouse for chickadees. You will need 24 sticks for the floor. Put 12 together one way and then lay 12 the other on top of the first layer. And, 24 sticks for each side. Put these together the same way as the floor. For the roof you will need 12 sticks. The back and front will be made from styrofoam. Make the hole in the front of the styrofoam 1½".

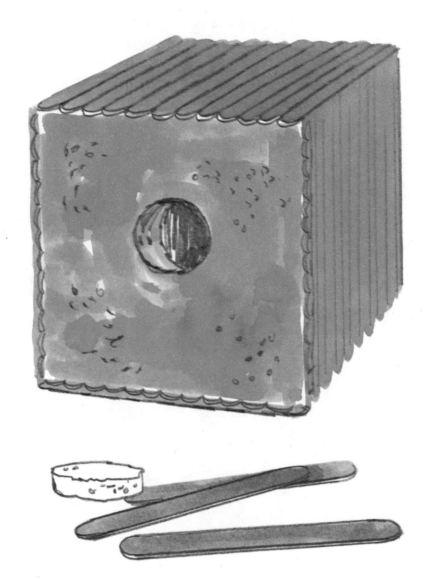

Now, let's make a birdhouse for wrens. You will need 10 popsicle sticks for the floor. Cut styrofoam for the front and back. Cut it in a triangle making the bottom 4 inches long. Glue the bottom of the styrofoam to the popsicle sticks. Glue popsicle sticks down each side for the roof. The hole in your styrofoam front should be 1 inch. Don't worry if the birds do not flock around your feeders and houses as soon as you are finished with them. Birds are shy and will just sit and watch until they are sure it is safe for them.

The best time to place birdfeeders outside is in the fall. Once you have birds eating from your feeder do not stop putting the food out each day until late spring when the birds will be able to find their own food. If you do stop, the birds might die without food.

Your birdhouses will have the most activity in the spring. The birds will begin to build nests. And you can look for baby birds.

Seed mixtures will attract all kinds of birds. And you can include bread crumbs, donut crumbs or cookie crumbs. You might also try berries, nuts and fruits from time to time. Something else that you can put in your birdfeeder is suet or beef fat. Try to keep your birdfeeder clean.

Birds also like water. They use it to drink and to take baths. Put a small plastic dish, like one that margarine comes in, inside your birdfeeder on a warm day and watch the fun a bird has taking a bath. Don't use a pan that is made of metal or tin. It will become too hot from the sun. Also, don't put too much water in your dish.

Even though you had fun making the feeders and houses, I'm sure you will enjoy watching the birds use what you have made for them.

# how to have fun

creative
craft
books